At the Beach

by Maryellen Gregoire

Nancy E. Harris, M.Ed—Reading
National Reading Consultant

capstone classroom
Heinemann Raintree • Red Brick Learning
division of Capstone

Many animals live at the beach.

Many animals move at the beach.

I see a crab walking on the sand.

The crab has a flat head.
It has red eyes.

I see a flamingo walking on the sand.

The flamingo has a pink head. It has small eyes.

I see a sea lion sitting on the beach.

The sea lion eats fish.
It eats big fish.

I see a penguin sitting on the beach.

The penguin eats fish.
It eats small fish.

I see a sea gull flying over the beach.

The sea gull eats fish.
It has a long bill to eat fish.

I see a pelican flying over the beach.

The pelican eats fish.
It has a big bill to eat fish.

How does a boy move at the beach?